Read & Respond

FOR KS2

SECTION 1
The BFG

Teachers' notes ....

SECTION 2
Guided reading

Teachers' notes 4

SECTION 3
Shared reading

Teachers' notes 7
Photocopiable extracts........................... 8

SECTION 4
Plot, character and setting

Activity notes 11
Photocopiable activities 15

SECTION 5
Talk about it

Activity notes 19
Photocopiable activities 22

SECTION 6
Get writing

Activity notes 25
Photocopiable activities 28

SECTION 7
Assessment

Teachers' notes and activity 31
Photocopiable activity 32

PAGE 1

Read & Respond

FOR KS2

Author: Jillian Powell

Editor: Victoria Lee

Assistant Editor: Rachel Mackinnon

Series Designer: Anna Oliwa

Design: Q2A Media

Illustrations: Quentin Blake

Text © 2007 Jillian Powell © 2007 Scholastic Ltd

Designed using Adobe InDesign

Published by Scholastic Ltd, Villiers House,
Clarendon Avenue, Leamington Spa,
Warwickshire CV32 5PR

www.scholastic.co.uk

Printed by Bell & Bain
1 2 3 4 5 6 7 8 9   7 8 9 0 1 2 3 4 5 6

British Library Cataloguing-in-Publication Data
A catalogue record for this book is available from the British
Library.
ISBN 0-439-94516-X   ISBN 978-0439-94516-5

Acknowledgements
The publishers gratefully acknowledge permission to reproduce
the following copyright material: **David Higham Associates** for
the use of extracts from *The BFG* by Roald Dahl © 1982, Roald
Dahl Nominee Ltd. (1982, Jonathan Cape). **Penguin Group (UK)**
for the use of the front cover of *The BFG* by Roald Dahl © 2001,
Penguin Group (UK) (2001, Puffin Books). **A P Watt Limited** for
the use of illustrations from *The BFG* by Roald Dahl illustrations ©
1982, Quentin Blake (1982, Jonathan Cape).
Every effort has been made to trace copyright holders for the works
reproduced in this book, and the publishers apologise for any
inadvertent omissions.

The BFG

About the book

The BFG was a character invented by Roald Dahl for his own children. Dahl would sometimes climb a ladder up to their bedroom window when they were in bed, and push the curtains aside with a bamboo cane, as if he were the dream-blower come to visit them. The Big Friendly Giant first appeared in one of the stories that Danny's father told him in *Danny the Champion of the World* (1975). Sophie, the other main character in *The BFG*, is named after his granddaughter, the model, Sophie Dahl.

The book, with illustrations by Quentin Blake, was first published in 1982. It tells the story of a lovable friendly giant who is accidentally spotted by a little orphan girl, Sophie, while on his dream-blowing mission. He carries her away to his home and the two become friends and allies in the fight against the evil, man-eating giants with whom he shares Giant Country. The story is both adventure and fairy tale, with elements of each intertwined in a tale of quest and glory. It carries echoes of familiar folk tales with references to the giant and Jack, from 'Jack and the Beanstalk', and has a fairy-tale happy ending in which good triumphs over evil, and all get their just deserts.

About the author

Roald Dahl was born in Llandaff, Wales in 1916. As a boy, he loved stories and books. He kept a secret diary from the age of eight in a tin hidden in a 'conker tree' in the garden. His parents were Norwegian, and his mother would

tell him and his sister stories of trolls and other mythical creatures. At school, he was good at sports, but his English teacher wrote that he was 'incapable of marshalling his thoughts on paper'. Dahl later told the story of his childhood in his autobiography, *Boy*. During the Second World War (1939–45) he became a pilot in the RAF, but was shot down and invalided out in 1942. His first published work was an account of his wartime experiences.

In 1943 he wrote his first work for children, *The Gremlins*. By the 1960s, he was married with children and was living in a house in Buckinghamshire, where he wrote in a hut at the bottom of the garden. He became famous for often macabre short stories, with a twist at the end, and increasingly for his books for children. He once said: 'I only write about things that are exciting or funny. Children know I'm on their side.'

His children's books have been translated into 34 languages: over a million copies are sold in the UK each year. Dahl died in 1990 at the age of 74.

Facts and figures
The BFG:
Author: Roald Dahl
Illustrations by: Quentin Blake
First published: 1982
Winner of the Children's Book Award and awards in Germany and Norway
Winner of the Good Book Guide Best Books of the Past 20 Years
Adapted into a comic strip in the *Mail on Sunday* 1986
Adapted into an animated film 1989
Adapted into a play by David Wood

Guided reading

First reading

Look together at the cover of *The BFG*. Ask the children what it suggests about the book inside. (It is fun, probably funny, and it has fairy-tale characters.) Ask them what they know about the author Roald Dahl, and if they have read any other books by him. What would they expect a book by Roald Dahl to be like? (Funny, a bit rude and exciting, perhaps.) Next, read the back-cover blurb, then the 'List of Characters'. Ask what more we learn about the story from these. (It has characters from the human and giant worlds, a friendship between Sophie and the BFG and some nasty, evil-sounding giants.) Finally, scan through the chapter headings and ask the children what the story will be like. (Adventure, scary, fantasy.)

At this stage you may discover some children know the story, either through reading the book or seeing the film. Discuss the importance of not spoiling the story for others.

'The Witching Hour' to 'Snozzcumbers'

Read the first chapter and encourage the children to describe the mood the writer creates. Does it make them want to read on and, if so, why? Continue reading to the end of 'The Cave'. Ask the children to recap what has happened to Sophie and where she finds herself. Read on through the next two chapters; then ask the children what Sophie has now learned that changes things.

Look at the picture of Sophie with the BFG in 'The Giants'. Let the children compare it with earlier pictures of the BFG. How does he look different now, and how does the picture reflect the story? (He seemed scary but is really a kind and friendly giant.) What is the problem that faces them in Giant Country? (The exploits of the man-eating giants.) Read to the end of 'Snozzcombers' and ask the children what else they have learned about the BFG (for example: the way he talks, his super-sensitive ears, what he eats).

'The Bloodbottler' to 'The Royal Breakfast'

Continue to read, pausing at the illustration of the Bloodbottler and the BFG. How does the BFG look now? (Quite small and vulnerable.) How do he and Sophie trick the Bloodbottler? (Sophie hides inside the snozzcumber.) At the end of the chapter, ask the children if they have any ideas on how Sophie and the BFG can stop the man-eating giants. What do the giants have in their favour? (Their size and strength, and there are nine of them.) What might their weakness be? (They are not so clever as Sophie and the BFG.) Read on to the end of 'A Trogglehumper for the Fleshlumpeater'. Ask the children where Sophie's adventure has taken her now (to Dream Country) and how the BFG tricks the man-eating giants this time. (By giving the Fleshlumpeater a nightmare.) Can the children remember the BFG's names for good dreams and bad dreams? (Phizzwizard and trogglehumper.) Read the next two chapters. Ask the children to explain what Sophie's plan is. Who are they going to ask for help?

Continue to the end of 'The Palace'. Ask the children why they think Sophie has to do the next bit of the plan. (The Queen might be terrified to see the BFG.) Read to the end of 'The Royal Breakfast'. What evidence does the Queen now have that Sophie and the BFG are telling the truth? (The newspaper reports and the Queen's telephone calls around the world.)

'The Plan' to the end

Read the next two chapters, as far as '…like gunfire in a battle.' Look at the illustration together and ask the children what the Army is planning to do. What is the risk or danger of the plan? (The giants might wake up.) Allude to *Gulliver's Travels* by Jonathan Swift, telling the children that Gulliver gets tied up by the tiny people of Lilliput, much as the BFG is planning to have the man-eating giants tied up. Carry on to the end of the chapter and ask the children to précis what has happened.

Finish the story together and ask the children to summarise the outcome for the main characters.

Guided reading

What sort of ending does the story have? (A happy, fairy-tale ending.)

Second reading

Read the first chapter together. Ask the children what we learn about Sophie. (She wears glasses and lives in a children's home.) Direct them to the words in italics. Which words are repeated more than once? What effect does this have? (It builds suspense and mystery.) Read on through the second chapter. How are capital letters used in a special way in this chapter? (To highlight key descriptions.)

Continue to the end of 'The Cave'. Can the children say what questions are left unanswered by the end of this chapter? (*Who is the giant? Where has he taken Sophie? What is he going to do with her? What is in the jars, and what was he using the trumpet for?*) Point out that these are all page-turners – they 'hook' the reader in and make us want to read on.

Sophie and the BFG

Read the next chapter together, 'The BFG'. What does Sophie find out about the BFG and the place where he lives? Invite the children to pick out unusual words that he uses: real words (for example, gobble), words that are made up (for example, wopsey whiffling), and words that are muddled versions of real words (for example, cannybull).

Carry on to the end of 'The Marvellous Ears'. What special skills or features does the BFG have, and what does he do? Ask the children to summarise what Sophie learns about dreams.

Read to the end of 'The Bloodbottler'. Ask the children to describe the ways in which the BFG is different from the other giants in Giant Country. What would he and Sophie like to do? (Make the other giants disappear.)

Remind the children of fairy stories like 'Snow White' and 'Cinderella'. Can they recall good and bad characters from these familiar stories? Which are the good and bad characters in *The BFG* and what problem faces the good characters?

Dreams

Continue reading as far as 'Dream-Catching'. Ask the children what the BFG reveals to Sophie about humans. What do the children think the author's message is here? (He points out how cruel humans can be to each other.)

Read the next two chapters. Ask the children if they have ever thought about where dreams come from. Discuss any dreams they can remember, and anything they think might have triggered them. Tell the children that for some Aboriginal or native peoples, such as Amerindian tribes, dreams are an important part of their legends and culture. Amerindians believe that dreams are sent from sacred spirits. If possible, show the children a picture of a Native American dream-catcher, which were traditionally hung up to protect children from nightmares.

Together, read 'Dreams'. Pause at the mention of Dahl's Chickens and ask the children who the BFG means (Charles Dickens), and if they can explain the writer's joke in the wordplay.

The great plan

Read 'The Great Plan'. Ask the children why the BFG is frightened of going to London at first? What does he think will happen to him? Read on through the next two chapters. Can the children remember the first time the BFG carries Sophie on a journey? How is this journey different? (Sophie trusts the BFG and they are on a mission together.) Read at pace the next two chapters. Ask the children how Sophie knows the plan is starting to work. (The Queen is having the dream.) Why is the maid shocked by what the Queen says? (She has already read about it in the morning newspapers.)

Continue through 'The Royal Breakfast'. Pause at the description of Sophie's clothes and ask the children how the sapphire brooch is significant. (Sophie will use it to trick the Fleshlumpeater.) How does the BFG embarrass Sophie? (Talking about whizzpopping in front of the Queen.)

Read 'The Plan'. Ask the children how long

Guided reading

the man-eating giants have been stealing people away to eat them. (Ten years.) What do the Army and Air Force Heads want to do to stop them? (Kill them.) What does the BFG suggest instead? (Capturing them.)

The big friendly giant

Read at pace 'Capture!' Ask the children what happens that might ruin the plan. (The Fleshlumpeater wakes up.) How do Sophie and the BFG get the upper hand again? (They trick him.) Ask the children to explain how the giants are taken back to England (carried under helicopters) and what else the Army carries back. (The BFG's dream collection.)

Read together the last chapters. Ask the children who the writer says wrote the book. (The BFG.) Tell them that the author, Roald Dahl, used to pretend to be a dream-blower for his own children, climbing a ladder to tap at their bedroom window as if he were the BFG. Suggest that Roald Dahl might have seen himself as a BFG-type character – he was very tall (about two metres), sometimes a bit scruffily dressed, and was kind and caring towards children.

Finally, discuss the book generally with the children. Did they enjoy reading it, and, if so, why? Review the way Quentin Blake has illustrated the book. Does Quentin Blake's style suit the story? Why?

Shared reading

Extract 1

- Read an enlarged copy of Extract 1. Ask the children to explain what a snozzcumber might be. (A cucumber.)
- Can they work out about how long it is meant to be? (One and a half times a man's height, so about 2.5–3m.)
- Highlight 'girth' and 'perambulator'. Can the children suggest alternative words?
- Underline the verbs that the BFG uses to describe how he feels about the snozzcumbers. (Squoggle, mispise, dispunge.) Ask the children to suggest some words to replace them. What sort of feeling do they all convey? (Disgust.)
- Which saying does the BFG get muddled up with? (Skin and bones.) Check the children understand the expression. Does the BFG's version work in its own way? (He might be so thin and hungry he would be groaning all the time.)
- Ask the children to explain how the BFG's language gets 'a little squiggly'. (He mixes up sayings and muddles words and verb tenses.) Challenge them to find examples in the extract.

Extract 2

- Read Extract 2 together.
- Ask the children to explain what is in the jar. (A dream.) How does the BFG catch dreams and pass them on? Remind the children of 'dream-catcher' nets, such as the Amerindian peoples make.
- Where do the children think dreams come from? Discuss that sometimes they seem to relate to things that have happened in the day and that some scientists study both sleeping and dreaming.
- Circle the word 'translucent' and challenge the children to come up with another word or phrase to replace it. Underline the present participles 'shimmering', 'pulsing' and 'breathing'. Which is being used as an adjective? (Shimmering.) Which as verbs? (Pulsing and breathing.)
- Invite the children to explain what the BFG implies by the comparison with the north wind. Can they think of other ways that he disturbs Sophie's ideas in the book? (By what he says about humans killing each other, and how long humans spend sleeping.)

Extract 3

- Read an enlarged copy of Extract 3.
- Ask the children where Sophie is sleeping. (In the BFG's ear.) Which country are they in – Giant or Human, and how does the reader know? (Human, because it is green, and has mountains and forests.) Can they remember the colours of Giant Country? (A yellow wasteland with blue rocks.)
- Why do they think the BFG turns his head so suddenly? (He hears the giants coming with his super-sensitive ears.) He points with the trumpet – can the children explain what he normally uses it for? (Blowing dreams.)
- Underline the sentence in direct speech and revise alliteration. Can the children think of any other words beginning with 'g' that the BFG could use about the man-eating giants?
- Ask the children what the giants have been doing. Circle the word 'pack' and ask them what else it could be used for, and what connotations it carries here. (A pack of wolves roaming together to find prey.)

Extract 1

The BFG flung open a massive cupboard and took out the weirdest-looking thing Sophie had ever seen. It was about half as long again as an ordinary man but was much thicker. It was as thick around its girth

as a perambulator. It was black with white stripes along its length. And it was covered all over with coarse knobbles.

'Here is the repulsant snozzcumber!' cried the BFG, waving it about. 'I squoggle it! I mispise it! I dispunge it! But because I is refusing to gobble up human beans like the other giants, I must spend my life guzzling up icky-poo snozzcumbers instead. If I don't, I will be nothing but skin and groans.'

'You mean skin and *bones*,' Sophie said.

'I *know* it is bones,' the BFG said. 'But please understand that I cannot be helping it if I sometimes is saying things a little squiggly. I is trying my very best all the time.' The Big Friendly Giant looked suddenly so forlorn that Sophie got quite upset.

'I'm sorry,' she said. 'I didn't mean to be rude.'

'There never was any schools to teach me talking in Giant Country,' the BFG said sadly.

'But couldn't your mother have taught you?' Sophie asked.

'My *mother*!' cried the BFG. 'Giants don't have mothers! Surely you is knowing *that*.'

'I did *not* know that,' Sophie said.

'Whoever heard of a *woman* giant!' shouted the BFG, waving the snozzcumber around his head like a lasso. 'There never was a woman giant! And there never will be one. Giants is always men!'

Illustration © Quentin Blake

Extract 2

Sophie peered into the jar and there, sure enough, she saw the faint translucent outline of something about the size of a hen's egg. There was just a touch of colour in it, a pale  sea-green, soft and shimmering and very beautiful. There it lay, this small oblong sea-green jellyish thing, at the bottom of the jar, quite peaceful, but pulsing gently, the whole of it moving in and out ever so slightly, as though it were breathing.

'It's moving!' Sophie cried. 'It's alive!'

'Of course it's alive.'

'What will you feed it on?' Sophie asked.

'It is not needing any food,' the BFG told her.

'That's cruel,' Sophie said. 'Everything alive needs food of some sort. Even trees and plants.'

'The north wind is alive,' the BFG said. 'It is moving. It touches you on the cheek and on the hands. But nobody is feeding it.'

Sophie was silent. This extraordinary giant was disturbing her ideas. He seemed to be leading her towards mysteries that were beyond her understanding.

'A dream is not needing anything,' the BFG went on. 'If it is a good one, it is waiting peaceably for ever until it is released and allowed to do its job. If it is a bad one, it is always fighting to get out.'

The BFG stood up and walked over to one of the many shelves and placed the latest jar among the thousands of others.

'Please can I see some of the other dreams?' Sophie asked him.

Illustration © Quentin Blake

Extract 3

Sophie had not slept for a long time. She was very tired. She was also warm and comfortable. She dozed off.

She didn't know how long she slept, but when she woke up again and looked out over the edge of the ear, the landscape had changed completely. They were in a green country now, with mountains and forests. It was still dark but the moon was shining as brightly as ever.

Suddenly and without slowing his pace, the BFG turned his head sharply to the left. For the first time during the entire journey he spoke a few words. 'Look quick-quick over there,' he said, pointing his long trumpet.

Sophie looked in the direction he was pointing. Through the murky darkness all she saw at first was a great cloud of dust about three hundred yards away.

'Those is the other giants all galloping back home after their guzzle,' the BFG said.

Then Sophie saw them. In the light of the moon, she saw all nine of those monstrous half-naked brutes thundering across the landscape together. They were galloping in a pack, their necks craned forward, their arms bent at the elbows, and worst of all, their stomachs bulging. The strides they took were incredible. Their speed was unbelievable. Their feet pounded and thundered on the ground and left a great sheet of dust behind them. But in ten seconds they were gone.

Illustration © Quentin Blake

Plot, character and setting

Mixing the story

> **Objective:** To map out the main stages of the story.
> **What you need:** Copies of *The BFG*, flipchart or board, individual whiteboards and pens, photocopiable page 15, scissors, glue, pencils, paper.

What to do
● Re-read the first two chapters together. Ask the children what happens because Sophie gets out of bed. (The BFG spots her, and kidnaps her.) What might have happened if she had stayed in bed? (Sophie might not have met him.)
● Ask the children to suggest all the things that happen as a result of this meeting. (For example the discovery of the other giants.)
● In pairs, ask the children to refer to the story and make a list on their individual whiteboards of all the things in the book that Sophie and the BFG plan and do together.

● Afterwards, bring the class back together and discuss which things are most important in driving the plot. (For example, Sophie seeing the BFG.) Which things could be removed without changing the outcome? (For example, the BFG blowing dreams into the Goochey children's bedroom.) Which things are vital for the story? (For example, the man-eating giants.) If required, make notes on the board.
● Hand out the photocopiable sheet and ask the children to fill in the boxes, then cut them out and paste onto paper in the correct order.

> **Differentiation**
> **For older/more confident children:** Ask the children to choose the most significant boxes on the sheet and arrange them into a flow chart.
> **For younger/less confident children:** Encourage the children to think of any other significant elements in the plot and add them to the photocopiable sheet.

The witching hour

> **Objective:** To understand how settings influence events and incidents in stories and how they affect characters' behaviour.
> **What you need:** Copies of *The BFG*, flipchart or board, writing materials, individual whiteboards and pens.

What to do
● Read at pace the opening chapter of *The BFG*.
● Invite the children to scan the chapter and list, on individual whiteboards, all the things they can about when this scene takes place, and what sort of night it is. (It is the middle of the night; it is moonlit, very silent and still.)
● Now ask them to list some adjectives that the writer uses to describe how things look or feel to Sophie. (Witching, deathly, silvery, ghostly, misty.) What do the children associate with

moonlight? (Night, ghosts, magic.) Can the children suggest some adjectives to describe the mood these words and images create? (Eerie, mysterious, creepy.)
● Ask the children what is keeping Sophie awake. (The moonbeam.) What makes her get out of bed? (She thinks she will not sleep unless she closes the curtains.) What happens as a result? (She sees the BFG.)
● Encourage the children to recall any other scenes that take place in the story at night-time, and why they happen then. (The journey to London, so the BFG won't be seen.)

> **Differentiation**
> **For older/more confident children:** Ask the children to consider another setting in the story in the same way.
> **For younger/less confident children:** Let the children write a plan for a creepy scene in a book or movie.

Plot, character and setting

Which country?

Objective: To understand how writers create imaginary worlds, and to show how the writer has evoked them through detail.
What you need: Copies of *The BFG*, flipchart or board, individual whiteboards and pens.
Cross-curricular links: Geography.

What to do
- Read the beginning of 'The Cave' together. Ask the children where Sophie and the BFG are when they reach the 'desolate wasteland that was not quite of this earth'. (Giant Country.)
- Encourage the children to pick out its main features and write these on the board. Prompt them with questions, for example: *Is the land flat or hilly?*
- Challenge the children to name the three different 'countries' in the book. (Human, Giant and Dream.) Write headings for them on the board.

- Divide the children into three groups and assign each a country. Ask the groups to scan the book looking for the main features of their country, including details of sounds, as well as sights. (For example, the snoring of the giants.) Afterwards, bring the class together and consolidate their suggestions under the headings.
- Ask the children how they imagine the countries relate to each other geographically. When the BFG is travelling, what seems to separate the different countries? (He crosses mountains or oceans as he runs.)
- As a class, let the children suggest some adjectives to describe each country.

Differentiation
For older/more confident children: Ask the children to write a descriptive passage about Giant or Dream Country.
For younger/less confident children: Let the children paint Giant or Dream Country, based on the text.

Nice and jumbly

Objective: To investigate how characters are built up from details.
What you need: Copies of *The BFG*, flipchart or board, individual whiteboards and pens, photocopiable page 16.

What to do
- Read at pace the chapter, 'The BFG'. Write three headings on the board: 'Appearance', 'Character' and 'Language'. Ask the children to scan the text for everything they can find out about the BFG from this chapter.
- Challenge them to work in pairs to think of some more facts about the BFG to go under these headings. They can scan the whole story for ideas, making notes on individual whiteboards.
- Bring the class back together and add to the list on the board from the children's suggestions. Now

add another heading for 'Job and skills' and ask the children what special skills or attributes the BFG has, and what he does as a 'job'. (Super-sensitive ears, ability to run like the wind, is a dream-blower – he catches, mixes and blows dreams.)
- Next, ask the children how they would describe the BFG. As a whole group, discuss suitable adjectives and phrases.
- Hand out the photocopiable sheet to all the children to fill in independently.

Differentiation
For older/more confident children: Ask the children to extend their notes on the photocopiable sheet to write a descriptive passage about the BFG.
For younger/less confident children: Let the children take turns in pairs to write down one word describing the BFG, and find supporting evidence from the text.

Plot, character and setting

Storyboard

> **Objective:** To map out texts showing development and structure.
> **What you need:** Copies of *The BFG*, flipchart or board, photocopiable page 17, individual whiteboards and pens, pencils.
> **Cross-curricular links:** Art and design.

What to do

● Read the chapter called 'Capture!' together. Tell the children that they are going to imagine that they are filming this episode for a movie. Explain that movie scenes are often mapped out as a sequence of pictures – a storyboard. They are going to write notes to brief an illustrator for a storyboard relating the capture of the man-eating giants.
● In pairs, ask the children to make notes for the characters and props needed for their movie. One child can work on characters, and the other on props, and they can then collate their notes.

● Then, let them work together to make notes on the setting. Which places feature? (Britain and Giant Country.) How can they be depicted?
● Bring the class together and précis the key events in the chapter. Write suggestions on the board for the main stages in the action.
● Hand out the photocopiable sheet enlarged to A3 and ask the children to fill it in. They can work in pairs, using their notes and the back of the sheet if required.
● Finally, the children can compare their storyboard plans with the scenes that illustrate the chapter in the book. Have they chosen different scenes to illustrate and, if so, why?

> **Differentiation**
> **For older/more confident children:** The children could choose another episode to storyboard.
> **For younger/less confident children:** The children could draw the pictures for their partner's storyboard following their notes.

Happy endings

> **Objective:** To identify fairy-tale elements in a story.
> **What you need:** Copies of *The BFG*, writing materials, photocopiable page 18.

What to do

● Read the penultimate chapter, 'Feeding Time'. Ask the children how all the different characters fare – *How does the BFG's dream come true? How is Sophie rewarded? What is the fate of the man-eating giants?* Ask the children which other stories have happy endings like this. (Fairy tales.)
● Encourage the children to suggest any elements that familiar fairy tales have in common with *The BFG*. Which other fairy tale has a giant as one of the main characters? ('Jack and the Beanstalk'.) Which fairy tales feature an orphan or poor girl? ('Snow White', 'Cinderella'.) Which fairy tale has a greedy character who would eat

little girls? ('Red Riding Hood'.)
● Suggest that in most fairy tales there are good and bad characters. Who are they in *The BFG*?
● Elicit that, in fairy tales, the good characters usually face problems to resolve, or bad characters to overcome. What is the problem that Sophie and the BFG face, and how do they overcome it?
● Consider the magical element in many fairy tales and ask the children how magic appears in *The BFG*. (Dream-catching.)
● Hand out the photocopiable sheet for the children to complete.

> **Differentiation**
> **For older/more confident children:** Ask the children, in pairs, to write down how the BFG is different from most fairy-tale giants.
> **For younger/less confident children:** Let the children, in pairs, write about how the man-eating giants are typical fairy-tale characters.

Plot, character and setting

Unlikely friends

> **Objective:** To discuss characters' feelings and behaviour.
> **What you need:** Copies of *The BFG*, flipchart or board, writing materials.
> **Cross-curricular links:** PSHE.

What to do

● Ask the children to name the two main characters in the story (Sophie and the BFG). Why might they be unlikely friends? (One is a small girl, the other a giant man.) What brings them together in terms of the plot (a common desire to fight the man-eating giants) and in terms of character? (They have fun, and learn things from each other.)

● Challenge the children to say what Sophie learns from the BFG (for example, how to catch and mix dreams) and what he learns from her. (The correct word for things.)

● Write 'Sophie' and 'The BFG' as headings on the board and suggest adjectives describing each character. (For example: thoughtful, brave, clever for Sophie; kind, funny, gentle for the BFG.) Encourage the children to support their suggestions with reasons. (For example: Sophie is brave because she stabs the man-eating giant with her brooch.)

● Now ask the children to list the emotions that each character experiences during the story. (For example: terror, anger, pity, joy.) Write their suggestions on the board.

● Let the children work in pairs to think of episodes where the character experiences each emotion. Bring the class back together to discuss findings.

> **Differentiation**
> **For older/more confident children:** Ask the children to map out the course of Sophie's emotions by ordering the episodes.
> **For younger/less confident children:** Let the children make a chart of the BFG's likes and dislikes.

Little and large

> **Objective:** To investigate settings.
> **What you need:** Copies of *The BFG*, flipchart or board, paper and pens or pencils.
> **Cross-curricular links:** Mathematics; Design and technology.

What to do

● Read 'The Royal Breakfast' together. Ask the children to find in the text the human-scale objects used to prepare the BFG's breakfast. Write their suggestions on the board.

● Ask the children if they can think of any other stories which feature tiny or giant people. (*Alice in Wonderland* by Lewis Carroll, *The Borrowers* by Mary Norton, *Gulliver's Travels* by Jonathan Swift.)

● Discuss the ways these stories play with size and scale. (For example, in *Alice in Wonderland*, she shrinks and then grows.) What sort of imaginative ideas come into play? (Problems encountered; adaptation of objects.)

● Challenge the children to look around the classroom, and imagine they are seeing it in two different ways: they are big enough to fill the room; then they are just a few centimetres high. How would objects look different?

● Ask the children, in pairs, to think of designs for objects the BFG could use in the human world. For example: what might he use to brush his teeth? Let them draw and label some designs.

● Bring the class back together to discuss their ideas.

> **Differentiation**
> **For older/more confident children:** Ask the children to consider another familiar setting from a giant's perspective.
> **For younger/less confident children:** Let the children write down what the BFG will need in the human world and what he could use.

SECTION
4

Mixing the story

Explain how these feature in the story:

A suitcase	A garden spade and fork
An elephant	A sapphire brooch
A trumpet	Helicopters
A gigantic egg-beater	A giant net

Plot, character and setting

SECTION
4

Nice and jumbly

Write down some words to describe the BFG.

Where does he live?

What does he do?

What does he wear?

What does he eat and drink?

What special skills or features does he have?

Plot, character and setting

Storyboard

Write notes explaining what each scene in the storyboard should show. Include instructions for characters, setting and action. Add more boxes on the other side of the sheet if you need to.

Scene 1 Title: _____ Setting: _____ Characters: _____ _____ Action: _____ _____	**Scene 2** Title: _____ Setting: _____ Characters: _____ _____ Action: _____ _____
Scene 3 Title: _____ Setting: _____ Characters: _____ _____ Action: _____ _____	**Scene 4** Title: _____ Setting: _____ Characters: _____ _____ Action: _____ _____
Scene 5 Title: _____ Setting: _____ Characters: _____ _____ Action: _____ _____	**Scene 6** Title: _____ Setting: _____ Characters: _____ _____ Action: _____ _____

Happy endings

Which characters come from the real world?

_____

_____

_____

_____

_____

Which characters come from a fantasy or fairy-tale world?

_____

_____

_____

_____

_____

Write down some magical or fantastical objects or ideas that feature in the story.

_____

_____

_____

_____

_____

How does the story have a 'fairy-tale' ending?

_____

_____

_____

_____

_____

_____

Talk about it

Story themes

Objective: To identify typical story themes, for example, good over evil, weak over strong.
What you need: Copies of *The BFG*.
Cross-curricular links: PSHE; Citizenship.

What to do

● Read together from 'Journey to Dream Country', from: 'As soon as he was outside…' to: "'I didn't like that,' she said." Ask the children how the man-eating giants behave towards the BFG. Elicit that their behaviour is bullying. Why is he at their mercy? (He is smaller and weaker than they are.) How does the writer make us feel towards these giants, and what do we want to happen in the story?
● Ask the children to explain how the tables are turned on the man-eating giants. How do Sophie and the BFG each contribute to stop the giants? (Sophie hatches a plan, the BFG persuades the Queen, and leads the Army to the giants.)
● Can the children remember how Sophie and the BFG trick the Fleshlumpeater? (Sophie uses the brooch and the BFG tricks the Fleshlumpeater into thinking he has been bitten by a viper.)
● Encourage the children to suggest what the moral is at the end of the story. (Good characters overcoming bad, weak overcoming strong.) Challenge the children to think of other themes or morals that are hidden in *The BFG*, asking them to consider how human beings are portrayed.

Differentiation
For older/more confident children: Ask pairs to discuss what Sophie learns from the BFG and what he learns from her.
For younger/less confident children: Let pairs discuss other episodes when Sophie or the BFG trick the man-eating giants.

Page-turners

Objective: To analyse the features of a good opening.
What you need: Copies of *The BFG*, flipchart or board.

What to do

● Re-read the first chapter. Ask the children what we learn about Sophie from this text. (She is living in a children's home.) How is she feeling? What makes her seem vulnerable? (She cannot see anything without her glasses.)
● As a class, brainstorm adjectives to describe the mood of the first chapter and write suggestions on the board. Elicit that it is night, and everything is quiet. Draw attention to words and phrases like 'deathly still', 'pale and ghostly', and ask the children what sort of atmosphere these create. Can the children find a simile or metaphor used to describe the moonlight? (A silver blade.)
● Organise the children to work in groups of three or four and ask them to discuss what makes them want to continue to read the book, especially how the author creates suspense. (For example: the reader is left in suspense, wondering who or what is coming up the street, so turns the page to read the next chapter.)
● Encourage all the children to participate in the group discussion, both speaking clearly and listening carefully.

Differentiation
For older/more confident children: Ask pairs to discuss episodes where the writer creates suspense in the rest of the book. (For example, when the BFG plays a joke on the giants.)
For younger/less confident children: Let the children find one other exciting episode and explain, in pairs, how the writer builds suspense.

Talk about it

Funnybones

Objective: To compare forms or types of humour, for example, wordplay, word games, absurdities.
What you need: Copies of *The BFG*, flipchart or board, photocopiable page 22, pens or pencils.

What to do
● Read the section in 'The Royal Breakfast' beginning at: 'At the top of the ladder…' until: 'But she couldn't stop herself smiling.'
● Ask the children what they find funny about this episode. (The idea of 'whizzpopping' in front of the Queen; Sophie's embarrassment; the BFG's lack of social etiquette.)
● Encourage the children to suggest other aspects of the book that they find funny. (They can include words, sayings, episodes, illustrations.) Write their suggestions on the board.
● When you have a list, discuss the type of humour that they represent. (For example: the

BFG's muddled words could be classified as wordplay or word games; a funny episode might be slapstick; the tastes of the man-eating giants dark or gruesome, and 'whizzpopping' rude, silly or 'schoolboy' humour.) Write headings for each type of humour.
● Let the children work in pairs to fill in the photocopiable sheet. They should quote words or pictures from the text, or write summaries of any funny episodes or events.
● Finally, bring the class back together and discuss the children's findings.

Differention
For older/more confident children: Ask the children, in pairs, to invent other funny words or phrases the BFG might say.
For younger/less confident children: In groups of three or four, let the children read out episodes in the text and discuss what makes them laugh most.

Dream on

Objective: To use independent spelling strategies, and awareness of grammar.
What you need: Copies of *The BFG*, individual whiteboards and pens.

What to do
● Read the first boy's dream in 'Dreams' together. Ask the children if they can suggest which aspects of the text need correction. (Punctuation, person and tense of verbs, spelling.)
● Focus on the verbs. Ask the children what is wrong with the BFG's use of verbs. (He uses the third-person verb with the subject 'I'.) Ask individuals to say the correct form of verb as you look at the text together.
● In pairs, ask children to find, discuss and correct all the spelling mistakes in the passage. Making notes on their individual whiteboards.

● Bring the class back together. Remind the children that, at the end of the story, Sophie agrees to help the BFG with his English – and he improves so much, he is able to write the book!
● Ask the children to suggest other reasons why it is important to write clearly and correctly. (For example: written instructions could be misinterpreted; newspaper news could be misunderstood and so on.) In the discussion, lead the children to the conclusion that correct writing – spelling, grammar and punctuation – is necessary so that writing is easily understood.

Differentiation
For older/more confident children: Ask the children, in pairs, to choose another of the BFG's dream labels and discuss the corrections it needs.
For younger/less confident children: Put the children in mixed-ability pairs when discussing the passage.

Talk about it

Langwitch!

Objective: To use independent spelling strategies including building from other words with similar patterns and meanings.
What you need: Copies of *The BFG*, flipchart or board, photocopiable page 23, individual whiteboards and pens.

What to do

● Explain to the children that they are going to try spelling some of the BFG's wacky words. Read aloud and ask them to spell: delumptious, rotsome, maggotwise, phizzwizard, trogglehumper, human-beany tottlers, man-gobbling cannybull, disgusterous, skididdling, filthsome.
● Ask the class for their suggestions, and write them on the board, then correct them where necessary. Can the children remember what any of these words mean? Which words remind them of words they know? (For example: delicious, rotten, toddler, cannibal.)

● Challenge the children to identify the parts of speech. Do they think they are nouns, verbs or adjectives? How do they recognise them? (For example: an -ing or -ed ending for a verb, or -some for an adjective.) Draw the words together under headings and write their definitions alongside.
● Ask the children, in pairs, to pick out some more words from the text for their partner to spell. They should take turns, and then correct their spellings.
● Hand out the photocopiable sheet for the children to complete independently. Bring the class together and go through the answers.

Differentiation
For older/more confident children: Ask pairs to challenge each other with more words from the text, to decide which parts of speech they are and what they mean.
For younger/less confident children: Let pairs challenge each other to explain the meaning of their favourite words from the text.

Parallels

Objective: To compare and contrast works by the same author.
What you need: Copies of *The BFG* and *Matilda*, flipchart or board, photocopiable page 24, pencils.

What to do

● Tell the children they are going to compare *Matilda*, another story by Roald Dahl, with *The BFG*, and see what similarities they can find. Over a period of time, read the story of *Matilda* with the class.
● Ask the children for their reactions to *Matilda*. Which do they like best – *Matilda* or *The BFG*? Encourage them to give reasons. Can they think of any ways the stories are similar or different? Prompt them to consider character, plot and setting, and write some of their suggestions on the board.
● Focus on the characters. Ask the children to

name the two main characters in each story. What do Sophie and Matilda have in common? What do the BFG and Miss Honey have in common? What problems do the characters face in each story, and who helps them? (The Queen and Magnus' ghost.)
● Ask the children to describe the BFG's home. How does it compare with Miss Honey's home?
● Hand out the photocopiable sheet to each of the children to be completed independently. Afterwards, bring the class together to discuss findings.

Differentiation
For older/more confident children: Ask the children, in pairs, to discuss the good and bad characters in both stories.
For younger/less confident children: In pairs let the children discuss two characters from each story.

Talk about it

SECTION 5

Funnybones

Write three examples of funny words or sayings that the BFG uses in the book.

1 _____

2 _____

3 _____

Write three funny events that happen.

1 _____

2 _____

3 _____

Write an example of 'dark' humour in the story.

_____

_____

_____

_____

_____

_____

Write about your favourite funny bit in the story.

_____

_____

_____

_____

_____

_____

_____

Talk about it

Langwitch!

Write out the correct version of the BFG's sayings; then write the meaning of each underneath.

'I is only sleeping once in a blue baboon.'

_____

_____

'I think you is barking up the wrong dog.'

_____

_____

'They is always having fifty winks.'

_____

_____

'One right is not making two lefts.'

_____

_____

'I will be nothing but skin and groans.'

_____

_____

'You will be disappearing into a thick ear.'

_____

_____

'The answer to the maiden's hair.'

_____

_____

Talk about it

Parallels

	The BFG	*Matilda*
Who are the good characters?		
Who are the bad characters?		
What problems do the good characters face?		
How do they trick the enemy?		
Who helps them and how?		

Get writing

Journeys

Objective: To plot a sequence of episodes modelled on a known story, as a plan for writing.
What you need: Copies of *The BFG*, flipchart or board, writing materials, photocopiable page 28.
Cross-curricular links: Geography.

What to do

● Read together the third chapter, 'The Snatch'. Ask the children how Sophie is being carried. (Inside the blanket.) What can she see, hear or feel? How is she feeling?
● Challenge the children to think of other journeys in the story. Who makes journeys and why? Where are they going? Write their suggestions on the board.
● Ask the children to remember the different ways that Sophie travels. (In the BFG's pocket or ear.) How is she feeling on these journeys compared with that described in 'The Snatch'?

(No longer frightened that the BFG will harm her.)
● Invite the children to imagine that the BFG and Sophie make another journey – perhaps, they travel to one of the countries mentioned, for example: India or Jersey, or they go on a dream-blowing trip together. Explain that the children should concentrate on the journey there – how they travel and how they feel – rather than what happens when they arrive.
● Hand out the photocopiable sheet and encourage the children write a plan for this new journey.

Differentiation
For older/more confident children: Ask the children to use their plan to complete a short piece of writing about the journey.
For younger/less confident children: Let the children work in pairs to complete the photocopiable sheet.

Headline news

Objective: To develop a journalistic style of writing.
What you need: Copies of *The BFG*, writing materials, flipchart or board.
Cross-curricular links: ICT; Geography.

What to do

● Read together 'The Queen' from: 'Inside the room…' to: 'That's why I came over all queer, ma'am…'
● Invite the children to imagine the front pages of the newspapers that the maid has read, and ask volunteers to suggest the headlines. What else do they think the news reports might say? Encourage the children to think of the words a journalist might use. (For example: horrific, mysterious.) What sort of detail might the journalist provide? (Age and names of the children.)
● Ask the children who might be interviewed and quoted by the newspapers. Challenge them to think of some quotes.

● Remind the children that the newspapers do not mention the man-eating giants (as they are never seen), just the mysterious disappearance of children. They could invent some eyewitness accounts that add to the mystery, for example: the sound of distant thunder caused by the giants' feet.
● Challenge the children to write a newspaper report in a journalistic style, reporting the mysterious vanishing of the school children. The layout or design aspect could be developed as an ICT activity. As this is a potentially emotive subject, be sensitive to any individuals whom this could upset.

Differentiation
For older/more confident children: Ask the children to include references to the other countries that reported disappearing children.
For younger/less confident children: Let the children work in pairs to create the report.

Get writing

Dream recipe

Objective: To write instructional texts; to write a first-person account.
What you need: Copies of *The BFG*, flipchart or board, photocopiable page 29, writing materials.

What to do
● Read 'The Great Plan' from: 'Sophie was silent…' to: '…where the Big Friendly Giant is hiding.'
● Ask the children to summarise the ingredients in the dream that Sophie is suggesting for the Queen. Can they remember where and how the BFG finds and catches dreams? What does the BFG need to mix the different ingredients in a dream? How does he pass the dreams on?
● Tell the children they are going to try writing a recipe for their own dream. They can base it on a real dream they have had, or invent a good or bad dream. Discuss some ideas with the children, and write suggestions on the board for settings, characters and events for a good dream or a bad dream.
● Hand out the photocopiable sheets and ask the children to fill them in independently. Bring the class back together to discuss and assess their ideas.
● Encourage the children to use their recipe to write a short piece of narrative in the first person, describing having the dream, or waking up and recalling it.

Differentiation
For older/more confident children: Challenge the children to extend the writing into a longer piece, including both narrative and dialogue.
For younger/less confident children: Let the children write some more labels for their own invented dream mixes.

The Fleshlumpeater's story

Objective: To change point of view, for example, tell incident or describe a situation from the point of view of another character or perspective.
What you need: Copies of *The BFG*, flipchart or board, writing materials, individual whiteboards and pens.

What to do
● Read at pace from midway through 'Capture!' (from: 'The BFG, with Sophie now sitting…') to the end of 'Feeding Time'. Explain before you start reading that the children are going to think about the events from the point of view of the Fleshlumpeater.
● Ask the children to summarise what happens to the Fleshlumpeater and make a list of the key events.
● Let the children work in pairs, considering each event listed on the board from the point of view of the Fleshlumpeater. They should tell each event in the first person, for example: 'I was fast asleep when I felt something tugging at my arm…'
● Bring the class back together and review their ideas.
● Ask the children to imagine they are the Fleshlumpeater, trapped in the pit eating nothing but snozzcumbers. He is going to write a diary of what happened to him. They should first write the diary in correct English and then try translating part of it into 'Fleshlumpeater language', using his speech to help them. (For example: 'The rotsome human beans was attacking me.')

Differentiation
For older/more confident children: Ask the children to write a diary entry for the same events from Sophie's point of view.
For younger/less confident children: Provide a framework to help the children write the diary.

READ & RESPOND: Activities based on The BFG

Get writing

What's in a name?

> **Objective:** To write a sequence of poems linked by theme or form.
> **What you need:** Writing materials, flipchart or board, photocopiable page 30.

What to do

● Begin by explaining what an acronym is – with the BFG as an example. (A shortened form using the first letters of each word.) Explain that acronyms are often used for brand names as they are easily recognised and remembered.

● Challenge the children, in pairs, to think of some familiar acronyms, and then invent some of their own, for example, for a football team or a fashion brand. Bring the class back together and discuss their findings.

● Now introduce or revise the idea of acrostic poems – these are short poems that use the letters that make up a name or word to start each new line of the poem. Begin by writing an example on the board: THE BFG, and complete the line beginning with the 'F' – 'Frobscottle is his favourite drink.'

● As a group discuss some other ideas for things that could feature in an acrostic poem on the BFG. (For example: things he likes or dislikes, his big ears, his height.)

● Hand out the photocopiable sheet to each of the children and ask them to work independently to create their poem.

● Share some of the children's ideas.

> **Differentiation**
> **For older/more confident children:** Ask the children to try writing an acrostic poem about Sophie.
> **For younger/less confident children:** The children can write a short poem about the BFG in free form.

Whoppsy whiffling blurb

> **Objective:** To write a brief synopsis, for a back-cover blurb.
> **What you need:** Copies of *The BFG*, writing materials, flipchart or board, examples of books with good back-cover blurbs, individual whiteboards and pens.
> **Cross-curricular links:** Art and design.

What to do

● Show the children the example books you have collected. Consider these with the children, looking at the cover illustrations and blurbs. Which blurb makes the children want to read the story? Why?

● Explain that most books have a back-cover blurb that tells the reader something about the story. Tell the children that they are going to write their own blurb for *The BFG*.

● Divide the class into five groups. Ask the children to talk about their favourite episodes from the story and anything they particularly liked about the book.

● Bring the class back together and discuss findings.

● Focus on the key ideas that have emerged, such as: humour (the BFG's funny words) and the dream-blowing. Write the main points on the board.

● Challenge the children to try and summarise the plot in two or three sentences, making notes on their individual whiteboards. What happens to bring Sophie and the BFG together? What adventure do they go on?

● Hand out writing materials and ask the children to try and write their own back-cover blurb for *The BFG*, referring to their notes.

> **Differentiation**
> **For older/more confident children:** Let the children map out their own back-cover design, writing a brief for illustrations and text.
> **For younger/less confident children:** Ask the children to draw a back-cover design for *The BFG*.

Journeys

Sophie and the BFG go on a new journey.
Fill in the details below.

From:	To:

What is the purpose of their journey?

How do they travel?

How do they feel?

What do they see on the way

Illustration © Quentin Blake

SCHOLASTIC
www.scholastic.co.uk

Dream recipe

Ingredients

Characters

Setting

Plot

How to mix the dream:

What you need:

Method:

Write a label for your dream jar:

What's in a name?

Think of some words connected with the BFG beginning with each letter:

B

F

G

Write a short poem about the BFG starting a new line with each letter.

T _____

H _____

E _____

B _____

F _____

G _____

Assessment

Assessment advice

Assessment is an on-going process, allowing children and teachers to build on progress, and to identify and work on areas that require improvement. In *Read & Respond*, the children are asked to complete a range of activities. These involve speaking, listening, reading and writing skills. It is important to explain clearly, at the beginning of each lesson, the objective of the activity, and if possible to relate it to other literacy work or relevant subjects in the curriculum. This will help place objectives in context and consolidate learning objectives.

At the end of lessons, children should be encouraged to assess their own work against the objectives set, and decide how successful they were in a particular task, and which areas need improvement. For many tasks they will work in small groups or with a writing partner. They should also be encouraged to assess their partner's or group's work and offer constructive criticism to improve it. Teachers can assess progress on written work and on classroom observation of individual, paired and group work.

The BFG – the sequel

> **Objective:** To use different genres as models to write, for example, sequels, using appropriate conventions, language.
> **What you need:** Photocopiable page 32, flipchart or board, writing materials.

What to do
● Encourage the children to say if they enjoyed *The BFG* and, if so, why. Can they compare or contrast it with any other Roald Dahl stories (for example, *Matilda*) and say which they like best and why?
● Discuss together the genre of *The BFG*. Do the children think it is an adventure, a humorous story, a fantasy, a traditional story or a fairy tale? Ask them to identify the different elements of each within *The BFG* and write their suggestions under headings for each genre on the board.
● Ask the children if they can explain what a sequel is. Tell them that some books or films are so popular that they are followed by one or more sequels. Discuss some examples from well-

known books or films. Did the children enjoy them, and think they were as good or better than the original book or film? Are their any books or films that they enjoyed so much they would like to see a sequel?
● Challenge the children to think of an idea for a sequel to *The BFG*. What might happen in it? Prompt them, if necessary, with some suggestions. (For example: *What might happen if one or more of the man-eating giants escaped in London and the BFG and Sophie had catch them again?*)
● Ask the children to start by working in pairs and make a list of all the ingredients a sequel to *The BFG* would need. Then, bring the class back together to discuss their ideas. Write some headings on the board for different elements: for example, funny events, wordplay, an adventure.
● Let the children work on their own to complete the photocopiable sheet, using their knowledge of *The BFG*. They should first fill in the boxes on *The BFG*, then fill in the other boxes to plan out a sequel to the story.

The BFG – the sequel

	The BFG	My sequel
Who are the main characters?		
Describe the main settings.		
Summarise what happens in the story.		
How does the story end?		